Benjamin's Christmas Cookie Jar

By

Mary Peirce Bale

Illustrations

By

Mariah Grace

©Mary Peirce Bale
Colorado Springs, CO
All Rights Reserved

Illustrations by Mariah Grace

Published by
Little Mary Sunshine, LLC
6555 Ramrod Road
Colorado Springs, CO 80933
mary_poetgal@yahoo.com

Layout by Mary Peirce Bale
ISBN-10:06157710263

This book is dedicated to Benjamin, my darling grandson who loves to bake with his mommy, daddy and grandparents.

Benjamin's Christmas Cookie Jar

Benjamin's Christmas Cookie Jar

Since Benjamin was two

He developed many fun things to do.

He liked to build with Legos and read books.

Play hide and seek in cozy nooks.

He would help mommy when she had to bake.

He loved to mix the dough for cookies or cake.

One year Nana gave Benjamin a Christmas Cookie Jar.

It was one of Benjamin's favorite gifts by far.

Weeks before Christmas mommy and Benjamin would make a list of baking items needed.

"Daddy, daddy, please take me to the grocery store." He pleaded.

"What's the rush Benjamin" daddy asked?

Excited, Benjamin replied, "It's time to bake and to fill my cookie jar. I need to get it done really fast."

Daddy replied, "Okay Benjamin, we'll go tomorrow after we finish our chores.

It we have time we may even go to some toy stores."

For months the Santa Jar set way back on
the upper, pantry shelf.
It was empty without even cookie crumbs
alone all by itself.

During Christmas time when Santa's face
wore a big grin.
Baked treats usually filled up the jar to its
brim. As soon as the jar was empty Benjamin
would yell, "We need to make more cookies
and fill him up again."

Once in a while Benjamin would open the pantry door.

He would look up at the Christmas Cookie Jar. Sometimes he would climb up on the stool. Then lift the lid hoping to find a cookie he could bring to school.

Benjamin wondered isn't time yet to bake
cookies with mommy''
Benjamin remembered the first cookie he
tasted and it was quite yummy!

One evening Benjamin tugged at mommy's shirt and asked, "Mommy can we bake Christmas cookies today?"
Mommy replied, "No Benjamin Christmas is still many months away."
"But the Santa jar is empty." Benjamin cried.
"We will make cookies soon when I'm not so busy." Mommy sighed.

Benjamin walked away quite sad.
He wanted to talk this over with his dad.
Benjamin just didn't understand why it
seemed the cookie jar was empty most of the
year.
With that thought on his mind he shed a tear.

One morning mommy tapped a sleepy
Benjamin on the shoulder and said,
"Wake up son, hurry and get out of bed."
Rubbing sleep out of his eyes Benjamin asked,
"Why?"
"Did something fall out of the sky?"

Mommy said, "Today is cooking baking day."
Benjamin jumped out of bed.
Then he danced around the room shouting,
"Hooray, Hooray!"

As mommy walked to the kitchen she yelled,
"Put on your cookie shirt, old jeans and your
chef apron."
"Be quick now for we have much to do son."
By the time Benjamin got to the kitchen door.
The mixing bowls were out as well as the
flour.
Mommy said, "Please get out the cinnamon,
baking soda and baking powder."

Benjamin climbed up on the kitchen stool and watched mommy whip the eggs.

"Can I sift the flour now?" Benjamin Begged.

Mommy guided Benjamin's hand as they mixed in the sugar and vanilla.

Next Benjamin sifted in the flour.

Mommy thought Benjamin was such a helpful little fella!

"I'll get out the Christmas cookie cutters." Benjamin said.

Mommy whispered, "I have some special cookie cutters we will use instead."

Benjamin asked, "But why?"

Mommy replied, "We'll cut out stars, flags and kites we can eat but that won't fly.

"For it is almost time for the 4th of July."

Benjamin sobbed, "I thought we were making Christmas cookies to fill up the Santa jar."
Mommy answered, "With the extra dough we will make angels, Santa faces, a Christmas tree, bells and a big star."
Benjamin asked, "So we can bake different kinds of cookies during the year?"
Mommy smiled and said, "Of course we can Benjamin dear."

Benjamin wasn't very happy about this situation today.

He searched the draws for the Christmas cookie cutters anyway.

Benjamin realized cutting out all these cookie shapes could be fun.

It would take more time to decorate each one.

They cut out flags, Uncle Sam hats,
firecrackers, kites and stars
Santa faces, bells, reindeer, trees and they
made marzipan bars.
They placed the cutouts on cookie sheets and
set them on the oven racks to bake.
Benjamin kept peeking in the oven window.
Oh it was so hard to wait!

Mommy stood on the kitchen stool and reached for the Santa jar just as the oven timer went ding.

She set the jar down on the counter and pulled out the cookie sheets just as Benjamin started to sing.

As the cookies cooled Benjamin sang, O Little
Town of Bethlehem.

Mommy was putting cookies on a plate when
daddy walked in.

Benjamin grabbed daddy's arm and said,
"Look at all the cookies we made this
afternoon.

It was so much fun icing all the shapes and
singing a Christmas tune."

Daddy muttered, "Mum, mum."

After they ate some cookies they put the rest in Benjamin's Christmas Cookie Jar and filled it to the rim.
Benjamin thought baking Christmas and patriotic cookies in July was just fine with him!

Benjamin popped a Santa cookie in his mouth
wearing a big grin.
He knew it would be a while before the
Christmas baking time would begin.

Mommy told Benjamin that each month she would set aside a special baking day.
They would try out different recipes such as flower shapes in May.
Benjamin was happy that he and mommy could bake any time of year.

Then he opened the pantry door, smiled at the Christmas Cookie Jar full of good cheer!

Another day Benjamin held his cookie jar.
He wished his Nana didn't live so far.
But Nana was coming for a visit soon.
He knew they would bake a cake before noon!

www.ingramcontent.com/pod-product-compliance
Lightning Source LLC
Chambersburg PA
CBHW060606030426
42337CB00019B/3638